Sticky HISTORY BOOKS

GREEKS

GODS AND EMPTY HORSES

Written by Rosemary Border

Illustrated by Peter Rutherford and Peter Wilks

HENDERSON
PUBLISHING PLC

If you haven't found history much fun so far, it's probably because you got bogged down in the boring bits. History is like a kipper - you sometimes have to work hard to get at the tasty bits. Our old history master, Mr Salmon - inevitably nicknamed Old Fishface - was a good historian. He also knew a lot about kids; and that was what made him a good teacher. At the start of a lesson Old Fishface handed out fact sheets.

"If you learn this by heart you'll know enough about the ancient Greeks" (or Vikings, or Romans, or whatever) "to pass your exams. Now I'll tell you something really interesting." And he did. He gave us all the tasty bits.

Sometimes we were so spellbound by his tales that we didn't even hear the bell at the end of the lesson. I have forgotten almost everything in Old Fishface's fact sheets, but not his stories. I keep them in a compartment of my mind labelled Useless Information.

Sticky History is real history (I didn't make any of it up, honestly!) with all the boring bits taken out. A sort of fillet of history - no skin, no bones, just the tasty bits.

Rosemary Border 1995

WHO WERE THE GREEKS?

A tricky one this - 'the Greeks' were lots of different things in different places. There was no Greece as such, just a lot of small city-states. Athens and Sparta were not far apart geographically, but life in Athens was so completely different in every way from life in Sparta that they could just as well have been on opposite sides of the world. Sparta and Athens had completely different laws and customs. Sometimes they traded with one another, sometimes they were at war. That's what life was like in Ancient Greece about 500 to 300 BC.

This is Ancient Greece. The Greeks were great seamen. Their warships ruled the waves and their merchant ships traded around the Mediterranean and Black Sea. They spent much of their time driving off the Persians, who tried to invade by sea.

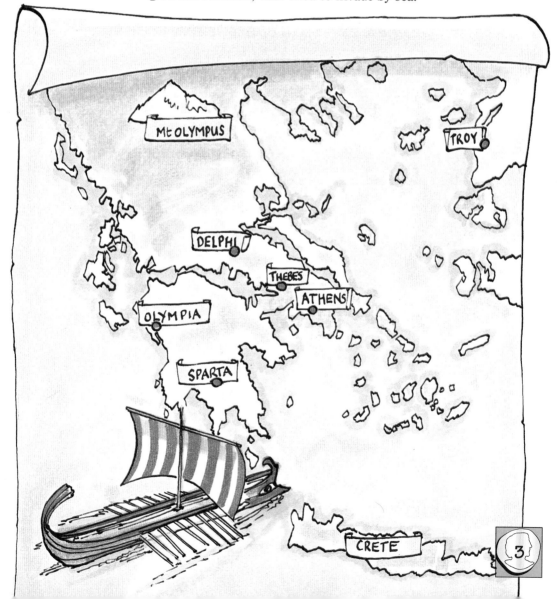

HOW DO WE KNOW ABOUT THE GREEKS?

To start with, the Greeks put up a lot of impressive buildings. Some are still in surprisingly good condition, even today. Others are in ruins. Surprise, surprise! You'd be even more surprised what the boffins can learn by studying what is left. Archaeologists *(that's an expert with a spade,)* dig about in the earth all over the Greek world. From the things they excavate, we slowly discover how these people once lived there.

The Ancient Greeks weren't any old bunch of peasants, oh, no! They had culture. And a lot of it. Greek carvings, paintings and mosaics often picture important events like battles which really took place. *(The Greeks loved a good battle!)* There are pictures which show them doing ordinary things, too, like brushing their teeth or gobbling up the Sunday roast.

Above all, the Greeks loved a good story. They made up loads, the more far-fetched the better. We call them myths and legends. Their best stories have been passed on for yonks. Big clay pots, and plates and even walls were often painted with pictures from myths and legends. Some of the old Greek yarns are pretty mixed up and difficult to understand. Perhaps, when the museum bloke put the broken pieces all back together, he put the pictures in the wrong order? That would explain a lot!

We got gods, we got culture, but we still ain't got no printing press!

4

We've learned a lot about clothes, furniture and everyday things from pictures on Greek pottery. Every tiny object in these pictures is closely studied. Then experts work out what any mystery objects were used for.

Then there was the writing. Fortunately, the Greeks loved to write about themselves. And about their adventures and their neighbours, too. Some very old languages, like Ancient Egyptian, were forgotten over the years, so it took scholars hundreds of years to decipher the writing in the pyramids. The Ancient Greek language was never forgotten because it was always used.

Many children went to school, even back in ancient Greece. Until quite recently, well educated people everywhere could read and write ancient Greek. Did you know that Grammar schools got their name because the chief subjects were Greek and Latin grammar? Chaps called scribes copied out the ancient books by hand, again and again, so that if the originals ever got lost, there were faithful copies.

USELESS INFORMATION:
A BIG BANG

The Parthenon, the big temple on the Acropolis above Athens, was in great shape right up until 1687. Yet another army was invading Greece at the time, and they decided to store their gunpowder inside it... Well, the Parthenon didn't look quite the same after that!

5

THE STORY OF GREECE ...

WELL, A SHORT STORY ACTUALLY. VERY SHORT.

Old Fishface would have put this on a fact sheet. It tells you where everything fits in.

BC AND AD

BC means Before Christ. AD means Anno Domini, which is Latin for In the Year of the Lord. If you say that Jesus Christ was born in 0 AD, you can set out the important dates in history along a time line. All the things we are concerned with in this book happened BC *(a mega long time ago!)*.

BC is like a countdown; five, four, three, two, one - so a battle in 100 BC happened 50 years before another battle in 50 BC. A person born in 400 BC, who lived to be 50, died in 350 BC. *Geddit?*

AD works the other way. 100 AD is later than 50 AD. A person born in 300 AD, who lived to be 50, died in 350 AD. *(You must get this bit, or how will you know how old you are?)*

BC

1,600 - 1,200	Mycenean Civilization in Greece
1193	Destruction of Troy by Greeks
1100	Dorians invade Greece (Homer calls this the Dark Ages)
776	First Olympic Games
490	Greeks defeat Persians at Battle of Marathon
480	Persians invade Greece - Athens is burned
479	Greeks defeat Persian army at Plataea
460	Athens and Sparta at war
447	Construction of Parthenon at Athens begins
431	Second Peloponnesian war between Athens and Sparta
404	Spartans capture Athens
356	Macedonians conquer Greece
332	Alexander the Great founds Alexandria, leading Greek city in Egypt
323	Death of Alexander - end of great age of Greece

Around 6000 BC, Stone Age hunters started farming instead of just trapping animals and picking wild fruits and grains.

From 1600 BC, a great civilisation grew up. These people were the Myceneans, who spoke an early sort of Greek. They fizzled out about the time of the Trojan War, in about 1100 BC.

What put pay to the Myceneans were a tribe called the Dorians. They invaded from the north in about 1100 BC. Homer, that most famous of all Greek poets, wrote about this period, calling it the Dark Ages. Which is appropriate, since Homer was blind.

Next, in the Archaic Period, there were a lot of changes. Kings were thrown out and leaders were elected by the people. Athens, now a city-state, grew to be its most powerful in the next 200 years. History boffs call that time the Classical Period.

THE THREAT FROM THE EAST

Now a long way away, in Asia Minor, lived some Greeks. Don't ask why. Perhaps they went to do a spot of trading, and decided not to come back. Anyway, in 499 BC, these Greeks got fed up with the rulers of the land, who were Persians. They had a revolt. *(That's when everyone runs around being revolting to each other.)* The good old Greeks back at home in Athens sent help, but the Persians had already stamped out the revolting Greeks and now it declared war on Athens. Seems to me they had a point, those Persians!

These Greeks are revolting!

MARATHON WELCOMES CAREFUL RUNNERS. SPARTA 140 miles

The Athenians were often scrapping with their Greek neighbours, the Spartans, but the two city-states forgot their differences, just for now, and joined forces against the Persians. The Greeks hammered the poor old Persians until the Persians decided they had had enough.

The modern Marathon was started in 1896 and is the distance between Marathon and Athens. Maybe the organisers thought 140 miles was too far...?

AREN'T WE EVER SO GRAND!

In Athens the next 50 years or so were a golden age of art and knowledge. Athens made friends with other city-states and together they were very powerful in Greece. In 432 BC the Parthenon, the great temple on the hill above Athens, was completed.

Now for the Hellenistic Period... In 336 BC Philip was assassinated and his son Alexander became king. Young Alex was a great bloke. He built up a huge empire, which his generals shared out between them when he died in 323 BC. Oops! It looks like things are beginning to fall apart.

> But sir, it's all Greek to me!

YOUR TIME'S UP, SPIRO!

> What do you mean you left your lunchbox on the roof?

But soon the boys were at it again! Sparta and Athens were busy fighting each other. This time it lasted from 431 BC to 404 BC. These were called the Peloponnesian Wars, 'cos that's where it all happened. Anyway, the Spartans defeated the Greeks and put in their own government. What an ego blow that must have been! Luckily for the Athenians, though, Spartan rule didn't last very long...

Meanwhile, in 356 BC, King Philip of Macedon in the north of Greece, was throwing his weight around. In fact, he was such a bruiser that he took over the whole of Greece. Look out, scholars! Here comes the end of Athens!

By now the Romans, a stroppy, energetic, ambitious people who had started out in Italy, were beating up their neighbours one by one and taking their land. First they took over the Greek colonies in Italy. Then they moved in on Greece itself. Many Greeks were taken to Italy as slaves. By 146 BC Greece was nothing more than a piece of Rome.

However, Greek language and culture remained alive and kicking. Educated Romans spoke and wrote Greek as well as Latin, and the Romans employed Greek scholars, businessmen and teachers. Most of the great Latin works were copied out by Greek scribes.

Homer and the Trojan Wars

Remember Homer? He's that Greek poet. He's especially famous for writing two especially long poems. The 'Iliad' tells the story of the Trojan Wars which began when Paris, son of King Priam of Troy, stole Helen *(the unbelievably beautiful wife of the Greek hero Menelaus)*. The war went on for 10 years and ended in the destruction and looting of Troy by the Greeks.

In the 'Odyssey', Homer tells the adventures of cunning Odysseus, on his way home from Troy to the Greek island of Ithaca.

The journey took him 10 years because he was such a rotten navigator. He kept losing his way, being blown off course and getting held up by shipwrecks and monsters, sorceresses and giants. He got home eventually and his old, flea-bitten, rheumaticky dog, who had been waiting for him all this time, wagged his tail and died at his feet.

Now you've learned a Greek word! The word odyssey has become part of our language, meaning a long, dangerous journey full of adventures.

Homer's Gruesome Bits

This kind of poetry is called epic poetry. Old Fishface used to say, "Homer is a great poet, but he needed a good editor. The paperback translation of the Iliad runs to over 400 pages; I reckon you could tell the story in 20 if you skipped most of the bloody bits." Here's a few gory highlights for you:

"Lycon struck the cone of Peneleos's plumed helmet and his sword broke off at the hilt. Then Peneleos hit Lycon on the neck behind the ear and his sword blade went right through. Nothing held but a piece of skin, and from that the head was hanging as Lycon sank to the ground..."

"The point of Thrasymedes's spear, striking the base of the arm, severed the ligaments and wrenched the bone right out..."

"And in his fury he severed Imbrius's head from his soft neck and with a swing sent it whirling like a ball through the crowd to drop in the dust at Hector's feet..."

"Meanwhile Idomenus struck Erymas on the mouth with his relentless bronze. The metal point passed right through his skull, under the brain, and smashed the white bones. His teeth were shattered; both his eyes were filled with blood; and he spurted blood through his nostrils and his gaping mouth. Then the black cloud of Death descended on him...'

THE TROJAN HORSE

After 10 years the Greeks got tired of camping outside the walls of Troy. They couldn't get into the city by force, so they cunningly constructed a monstrous horse made of wood. Under the horse's belly was a trapdoor, and inside there was enough space - just - for up to ten armed men to hide, provided they kept still and didn't fight among themselves.

While they were building the horse, the Greeks spread the rumour among their ranks that they were going to give up attacking Troy and sail home, and that the horse was an offering to the gods to bless their homeward voyage. Well, as Old Fishface used to say, there was no shortage of double agents to pass the word to the Trojans.

Now the Greeks did actually set sail, but only as far as a nearby island. The Trojans watched them leave, and they thought their luck had changed at last. But the Greeks just sailed round the island and anchored their ships on the other side, out of sight of Troy. The Trojans were overjoyed. They swarmed out of their city and danced for joy on the beach where the Greeks had camped for so long.

You may hear people use the term, "a Trojan Horse" even today. It represents a gift which is really a sort of trap. Even people who know nothing at all about ancient Greece have heard of the Trojan Horse (honest, they have).

And of course the Trojans saw the wooden horse. *(They could hardly miss it, it was quite large.)* "Oh look," said one Trojan genius, "they've left their horse behind. I've heard they built it as an offering to the gods, but of course it's far too big and heavy to ship home. Let's drag it into the city and set it up outside our own temple to bring us luck." Another Trojan shook his head. "Burn it, I say. I smell treachery." "Me too," said another. "There's a cunning plot here. Either there are warriors hiding inside, or the horse itself is a weapon of some kind, designed to bring about our downfall." He picked up a spear and hurled it at the horse's huge wooden belly, where it stuck, quivering.

Just then a Greek prisoner arrived, led by some shepherds. He had let them catch him, and he was part of the plot, but of course the Trojans did not know that.

The prisoner wept pitifully as he was dragged before King Priam of Troy. His name was Sinon and the Greeks had chosen him for his acting ability. The King turned to Sinon. "Now - why did the Greeks build this giant horse? Is it an offering to the gods, or an engine of war?"

"Beware of Greeks bearing gifts" is often quoted, too. Ask grown-ups in your family if they've heard of it. It means much the same; don't be fooled, don't trust the giver. Rum lot, those ancient Greeks!

Sinon took a deep breath and launched into his story of how the Greeks had built the horse as an offering to the gods to give them a safe journey home, and how the horse, if the Trojans took it into their city, would protect them too. Of course, not a word was true, but the Trojans had heard the rumours and they believed Sinon's lies. They heaved the horse up on rollers and fastened strong ropes around its neck and started to drag it through their gates. They stood the horse outside their temple, then spent the evening feasting to celebrate this wonderful gift.

That night, Sinon opened the secret trapdoor under the horse's belly and set free the hiding warriors, including the ever-so cunning Odysseus. They stabbed the sleeping sentries and opened the city gates to the Greek warriors who had returned and were waiting outside... And so, by cunning and treachery, the Greeks entered Troy.

This isn't actually Fishface's private version. It's from a Latin poem by Virgil called Aeneid, in case you'd like to read the whole thing - if you've got all year!

Spiro's Place

"Zis iz 'ow we bildee thee owse. We takee the stone from the mountain side. Bricks we make with mud. Good Greek mud. On the roof I put thee tiles. The clay, cook-ed in the oven. Very preetty."

Houses are simple but as the weather is usually fine in Greece, folk spend a lot of time out of doors. Spiro's wife is off to the public fountain to do a spot of washing. *(All this revolting and sparring with the Spartan's is grubby work.)* Mrs. Spiro nags her husband to install a well in their own courtyard, like the posh houses down the road. But Spiro likes the peace and quiet when his wife and daughters trudge off to the public water place.

Did you spot the altar in the middle of the courtyard? You have to keep in with the gods if you're a good Greek, so each family makes sacrifices of food and wine. A bit like leaving a glass of sherry and a mince pie for Father Christmas, perhaps.

Outside Spiro's door is a herm. Every home should have one. It's supposed to guard the house against evil spirits. Mrs. Spiro bought it from the garden centre, but Spiro reckons a rabied old wolf-dog would do a far better job.

15

Now it might seem odd, but inside most houses in Spiro's street, the men and women have separate living quarters. The ladies of the household spend hours toiling in the loom room to spin and weave linen and wool to make cloth.

The cellar is a cool place for storing food and wine, which is just as well as it can get jolly hot in Greece. Especially at midday, when Spiro decides he suddenly has to inspect his wine stores. He keeps it in pottery storage jars, called amphorae. Have you ever spotted a copy of one of these ancient Greek amphorae in a garden? They're all the rage. Which is what Mrs. Spiro is when she finds her husband snoring in the cellar, half an amphorae later!

USELESS INFORMATION: NO SOAP!

The ancient Greeks did not have soap, shower gel or any other bathtime aids. They rubbed their bodies with oil and scraped off the oil, dead skin, sweat, etc with a metal scraper called a strigil. Luvverly.

Spiro has two daughters. No-one wants to marry them, since they're both pretty ugly and Spiro is too mean to pay a dowry. *(Usually in Greece, the bride's dad coughs up some dosh to get his daughter married and off his hands.)* So Katiana and her sister Thesbida are stuck in their mum's kitchen.

The girls are endlessly making bread, which means grinding corn into flour and then making the dough. *(Still, they've got nice big muscles.)* The ovens are made of pottery, for baking, and charcoal fires are lit for cooking meat and vegetables.

The kitchen has no chimney - so the smoke has to find its way out through a hole in the roof.

POSH TOUCH

If you lived in ancient Greece, especially if you lived in Athens, then you had to keep up with the Joneses. Well, no, not them exactly! The Welsh hadn't yet escaped the shores of Wales. Your neighbours were more likely to be Mr Arakis or Mr Alexandros. Inside their houses, the main rooms have a patterned border painted all round the walls. It took a steady hand! The design most Greeks used was bunches of grapes, or flowers, or decorative Greek patterns. (You must have spotted those regular squared patterns somewhere before.) It was too hot for carpets, so the floors would be made of stone and, for the very rich, marble or even mosaic.

HOW TO MAKE MOSAIC

You need:

A flat floor
Some cement
A board to smooth the cement
Boxes and boxes of tesserae - tiny squares of different coloured stone and sometimes pottery or glass, one box for each colour

Plan your pattern.
Spread cement on the floor.
Smooth it with your board.
Get your tesserae ready.
Make your pattern, sticking each tessera in the damp cement. Oh - make sure you work your way towards the door. If you don't, you'll have to wait in a corner until the floor is dry enough to walk on!

THE ANCIENT GREEK CLOTHES SHOW

Originally, ladies wore a peplos tunic, held together with a pin. The pin came in handy for stabbing soldiers, so the Greek government decided to change the fashion and disarm the girls. The chiton tunic was the answer - no pins.

Both men and women wore the same kind of chiton tunic. Ladies had a choice of two styles.

Sometimes a woman would wear a binding across her chest or a belt around her waist. And some materials had patterns, either all over or just as a border. Light shawls were worn, with a brooch at the shoulder, just to look nice. But in cold weather women also wrapped themselves in huge cloaks like blankets.

In the early days, clothes were all made of either linen and wool. Later on, the Greeks traded with other lands. Silk and cotton from the East became available, but only to the wealthy Greeks.

Older men, and also younger men on special occasions, would wear longer tunics.
Sometimes, instead of a tunic, a large oblong piece of cloth called a himation would be worn. And young men sometimes wore just a short cloak called a chlamys. But for travelling they would wear a big cloak over a tunic.

Hairy Hellenics

Greek men usually wore their hair fairly short. Many wore beards until the Hellenistic Period, when beards began to go out of fashion. There was no steel, so razors were made of bronze, which did not keep its sharp edge very long. Most men were shaved by slaves or at the barber's shop, which was a great place to meet friends and chat.

Women wore their hair long in all sorts of different styles, with ribbons, pins, scarves and jewelled headbands. For a time, fair hair was fashionable, and many brunettes either had their hair dyed or wore wigs.

Shoes were not a high fashion item in ancient Greece. Many people just went barefoot. Sandals were common everyday wear, but both boots and shoes were sometimes worn. We know because archaeologists have found eyelets for shoelaces and studs for boots. Some fine ladies, however, wore built-up shoes, like the platform soles of the 1970s, to make them look taller.

As for children, they wore more or less what their parents did.

Some marvellous ancient Greek jewellery has been found. (So, remember, don't go to Greece without your metal detector!) The Greeks were very skilled gold and silversmiths. They also used enamelling and coloured, sometimes carved, stones. A lot of Greek women had their ears pierced so that they could wear elaborate drop earrings. And noble ladies often wore a kind of crown called a diadem.

USELESS INFORMATION:
LINEN AND WOOL

Wool, of course, comes from sheep or goats. Yes, even in ancient Greece, they were those little fluffy things with four legs at each corner. You've got it! BUT, did you know that linen comes from a plant called flax? You have to beat the stalks to get at the fibres, then spin the fibres into a long thread ready for weaving.

With wool, you have to comb the wool and wash it to get rid of any tangled or dirty bits, then spin the thread.

BABY, YOU'D BETTER BE TOUGH!

Growing up was tough in ancient Greece. Unless your father was a paid soldier or a trader, or a councillor in the city, you might have been very poor. Many families lived very simply then, growing a few crops if the earth nearby was fertile enough, or keeping goats for milk and cheese, if they lived in the rocky hills.

When a baby was born, the mother showed the child to its father. Sometimes, he refused to accept it, especially if it was a girl, who could not work the land or get a paid job as a soldier, or protect the family. Then the mother had to abandon the child on a hillside - sometimes in a pot, sometimes just wrapped in a cloth - to die or be eaten by wild animals.

The Spartans were violent people. They threw their unwanted babies off a mountain top. This was more likely to happen if the baby was a girl, or if it was weak and sickly, but some healthy boys were abandoned, too. Greek stories are full of baby boys who were left to die, but were taken in by kind shepherds and grew up to become mighty heroes.

In wealthy families, if a son was born, the family held a party. They showed the baby to the gods and gave it a name. The mother might not look after the child herself, but hand it to a nurse who would live with the family and look after the child.

AT SCHOOL IN ATHENS

Probably the best childhood to have was a boy's, in Athens. Then you got to go to school each day.
(It could be worse, much worse!)
No such luck for the girls, even in the rich city of Athens. Girls stayed at home and learned all the housewifely skills. This didn't mean baking nice cakes and hoovering the carpets, either! It was very hard work, every day of the year.

GIRLS - THIS IS YOUR LIFE!

- learn spinning and weaving, to make all the cloth for the family's clothes
- grind corn for bread
- cooking - a slow, messy business

OPEN YOUR TABLETS, BOYS!

The boys wrote on wooden tablets with a wax coating. They wrote with a stylus, a sort of stick with a point at one end and a flat bit at the other to rub out mistakes. When you had finished with what you had written, you just rubbed everything out and the tablet was ready to use again. Music was an important part of the school curriculum. Pupils learned to play the lyre, a kind of harp, and to sing. Sums were worked out on a sort of counting-frame called an abacus. The beads on the top row are worth 1. The ones on the middle row are worth 10. The ones on the bottom are worth 100.

WE HATE THAT MATHEMATICIAN

Greece is famous for its philosphers. Any idea what they were? Well, there's a clue in the question. They're thinkers, scholars like writers whose ideas became famous. But even these bright boys had some weird views. One Greek author said, "Teaching a woman to read is like giving extra poison to a snake".
Phew! Did he have a complex!
Yet some girls were lucky enough to learn to read and write. Their dad must have been a good guy!

A rich boy would have a slave called a pedagogue who went to school with him and carried his books!

"Now pay attention, you lot. My name is Mr Pythagoras. I'm a most important Greek mathematician. You'll have heard of me, no doubt.
What d'you mean, 'no'?
I'm the brainy fellow who thought up Pythagoras Theorum. Oh, well, never mind. Just tell your maths teacher you've met me. That should impress them!"

Old Pythagoras was indeed a bright spark. His theorum is used in maths today. He was also one of the first men to believe that the Earth was not flat, but a sphere.

STAND UP AND SPOUT

Older boys were taught public speaking. They had to learn big chunks of poetry by heart, to teach them how to use language in a rich and interesting way. Then they took part in debates and public speaking competitions. The Athenians did not think much of strong, silent heroes!

USELESS INFORMATION: A GREAT ORATOR

Demosthenes was a famous ancient Greek orator, or public speaker. It is said he practised by trying to speak clearly with pebbles in his mouth (don't try this at home in case you swallow them!) and making speeches on the seashore, trying to make himself heard against the booming waves.

HOW TO MAKE PAPYRUS

Cut papyrus reeds from the river bank.
Peel away the green outside. You can throw this away.
Slice the white pith lengthways into wafer-thin strips.
Lay one layer of strips on top of another. Layer 1 goes left to right, layer 2, top to bottom.
Pound the pith into sheets with a wooden hammer.
Polish your papyrus with a stone to make it smooth.

We get our word *paper* from *papyrus*, the Egyptian reed. It is quite different from parchment, which got its name from the Greek city of Pergamon, and was made from the skins of animals *(dead ones, we hope)*. Most of the great works of the ancient Greeks were written on papyrus. Modern paper is made mainly from wood pulp - trees that have been shredded and soaked until really soggy.

THE GREEK ABC

The word alphabet comes from the first two letters in the Greek ABC: Alpha and Beta.
You, too, could be a Greek scholar. How 'bout that!
Here is what Greek pupils were faced with:

Name	Capitals	Lower case	English
Alpha	A	α	a
Beta	B	β	b
Gamma	Γ	γ	g
Delta	Δ	δ	d
Epsilon	E	ε	e *(ey sound as in they)*
Zeta	Z	ζ	z
Eta	H	η	e *(i sound as in thin)*
Theta	Θ	θ	th
Iota	I	ι	i *(y sound as in why)*
Kappa	K	κ	k *(c)*
Lambda	Λ	λ	l
Mu	M	μ	m
Nu	N	ν	n
Xi	Ξ	ξ	x *(ks)*
Omicron	O	o	o
Pi	Π	π	p
Rho	P	ρ	r
Sigma	Σ	σ	s
Tau	T	τ	t
Upsilon	Y	υ	u *or* y
Phi	Φ	φ	ph, f
Chi	X	χ	ch *(as in loch)*
Psi	Ψ	ψ	ps
Omega	Ω	ω	Oo

USELESS INFORMATION - CLEVER CAT?

The Greek letter mu sounds like a cat.
There is a scholarly joke about this:
There was a young curate of Kew
Who kept a black cat in his pew.
He taught it to speak
Alphabetical Greek,
But it never got further than m (mu).

USELESS INFORMATION - ASK NO QUESTIONS

One Greek scholary type was called
Socrates. He used to ponder about
life in general - why?, who? where?
He asked endless questions and tried
to find reasons for things. A bit like
you when you were a small kid!
Trouble was, Socrates asked so many
questions, he began to get on people's
nerves. In the end, they condemned
him to death and gave him poison
Hemlock to drink. Poor chap!

23

GROWING UP IN SPARTA

You may have heard people describing something as Spartan. The word conjures up plain food, hard beds and cold showers at 6 am. Life in Sparta was much, much worse than that...

In Sparta, all children belonged to the state. *(Those that weren't left on hillsides, that is.)* If they survived to the age of 7, boys were taken away from their families and sent to a kind of boarding school. Knowing what you do about the Spartans, you can imagine life at one of these places:

well, if it's courage you're after

All Pedonome pupils will receive regular beatings. This teaches them courage. Regular competitions will be held to see who can suffer most without complaining. Names are entered on the school Honours Board for outstanding courage.

Welcome to The Pedonome

(That's Spartan for a boarding school.)

Our boys will be tough and fit to fight.
No beds are allowed –
our boys sleep on the ground.
No bedclothes are permitted.

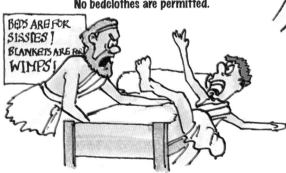

BEDS ARE FOR SISSIES!
BLANKETS ARE FOR WIMPS!

School meals are non-existent.
Boys have to steal to eat.
This teaches them to be cunning and clever.
If caught, we beat them.
(Not for stealing, but for getting caught.)

Music is an important part of the curriculum. Songs of war and love for our country are taught regularly.

The Spartans are Best, Down with the Rest

Dancing is also taught – not for balls and parties *(for wimps)* – but to make the boys strong and fast on their feet.

24

PEDONOME CLOTHES LIST

No clothes are worn AT ALL before the age of 12.

For over 12s:
1 tunic *(to be worn for a whole year)*
No shoes, winter or summer

WHAT ABOUT THE GIRLS?

Spartan girls did not go to boarding school, but they were brought up to be tough. All Spartan girls learned athletics and wrestling. And they were expected to be just as brave and tough as the boys.

Not surprisingly, the Athenians and the Spartans did not get on very well.

It's a foul!

Sport is an important part of any Spartan boy's education. Our boys run, box, play ball games and wrestle. Fouls are encouraged.

Take that daft hat off, Nikos!

All our boys are trained to become good soldiers.

Yaa, boo!

Hiss!

Aaargh!

SPORTY LOT

Sport was important. The Greeks had sports centres called gymnasiums where they could exercise and also meet friends. *(Sorry, no girls allowed.)* They went in for ball games including one which seems to have been rather like hockey.

NASTY PASTIMES

They also had some very unsporting pastimes - particularly if you were one of their domestic animals:

Men gathered around a hole in the ground, about 2 metres across, called the cockpit. Two cockerels were brought in. Sharp metal points called spurs, were tied to their legs. Then the two creatures were set on each other to fight. People around the ring would watch the fight and bet on the result. The two cocks would fight to the death.

Dogs suffered the same cruelty. It seems those macho ancient Greeks possessed a cowardly vicious streak!

The Greeks did play quieter games, too. There were board games, rather like draughts, and a version of jacks or five-stones, which you played with *(real)* knuckle-bones.

MUSIC

Although most Greeks had music lessons when they were young, almost all professional musicians were slaves, who were trained at special schools. Some were attached to one family; others could be hired from their owners for special occasions, like hiring a band or disco today. People planning a party could also hire jugglers, sword-dancers, acrobats, stand-up comics and storytellers.

USELESS INFORMATION: A PARTY GAME

A popular game at parties was cottabos. Here's the basic rules:

Take a cup of wine.
Drink most of the wine.
Choose a likely target - the stand-up comedian, perhaps?
Flick the wine at your chosen target. (Practise your aim at home; you don't want to flick wine all over your hostess's new dress.)

A Day at the Theatre

Going to the theatre was a great event. It started out as a festival to the god Dionysus (better known as the god of wine) and gradually developed into a sort of 10 day drama festival with awards for the best plays. There was only one performance of each play, so theatres had to be enormous to provide seats for everyone who wanted to see the show. Some theatres held up to 30,000 people. Semicircular open air theatres were the rule, with stone seats set into the hillside like steps. Some ancient Greek theatres are still being used, like the one at Epidaurus.

Making a Day of It

You would arrive at the theatre early in the morning and be prepared to stay all day. You brought a picnic lunch, you paid your entrance fee *(usually 2 obols; there were 6 obols to a drachma)*. The state had a sort of hardship fund for people who were really too poor to pay.

The judges sat in special carved chairs. *(Everyone else had to put up with hours on a cold stone slab.)* At the end of the festival the chief judge, who was also the priest of Dionysus, awarded laurel wreaths to the author of the best tragedy and the best comedy - a sort of Oscar.

Greek theatre was terrific value for money. You would see three tragedies *(no happy endings)* or three comedies *(nearly always a happy ending)* and a short farce *(a slapstick, messing about sort of play)*. Everyone in the audience knew the stories already, so there were no whodunnits.

All the actors wore masks. There were no actresses. Instead, women's parts were played by men in masks and long robes. Only a few actors had speaking parts. A group of players called the chorus made speeches to tell the audience what was going on...sort of like sports commentators on TV.

USELESS INFORMATION: YOU CAN HEAR A PIN DROP

The theatre at Epidaurus is so brilliantly constructed that you can sit at the very back and hear a coin drop on the stage. Theatres like this are said to have wonderful acoustics. (All very well, but can you SEE anything from that distance?)

A FAMOUS TRAGEDY

Oedipus the Tyrant was written by Sophocles. Oedipus was abandoned as a baby, so he never knew his parents. By a terrible twist of fate he killed his father and then married his mother. When he found out what he had done, he put out his own eyes with the pin of his mother's brooch.

What do you mean, you don't serve ice-cream?

A FAMOUS COMEDY

Comedies usually poked fun at daily life, politics, sex and the rich and famous.

In *Lysistrata*, the women of Greece get fed up with their men going to war all the time. So they get together and they all refuse to make love to their husbands unless they make peace.

USELESS INFORMATION – A FILLER

The word farce, which we now use for a funny play with everyone's trousers falling down, comes from the French farce meaning stuffing, as in stuffed tomatoes/chicken. The first farces were just there to fill in the time between the more serious plays.

29

THE OLYMPIC GAMES

Every 4 years the ancient Greeks held the Olympic games. Where? At Olympia, actually - what a coincidence. The games lasted for 5 days. They began sometime around 776 BC and were held in honour of the chief god, Zeus.
Only the men took part. Athletes came from all over Greece and even from the colonies in Italy and Asia Minor.

The Greeks were even keener on their Olympics than their fighting. They postponed wars for 3 months to allow people to travel safely to Olympia!

Olympia was a great showplace for tourists as well as a sports centre. There was a 13 metre gold and ivory statue of Zeus in the temple there. There were hotels for rich visitors; poorer ones just camped in the countryside around.

The athletes covered their bodies with oil as a protection against dust and sun. They didn't wear any trainers, vests or shorts - athletes competed naked and barefoot. The stadium held thousands of people. Most stood, but the judges had special seats at the front.

Here is part of the programme:

Running. The stadium is named after the stade, which was about 180 metres. There were 1 stade, 2 stade and 24 stade races. There was a special race for armed men. They had to wear helmets and greaves - leg guards - and carry shields.

Discus-throwing was a popular spectator sport. The discus was a flat disc made of bronze, like a heavy dinner plate.

Throwing the javelin was one skill which was useful in war as well as in sport. The javelin throwers were allowed to wrap a leather thong round their fingers to give them a better grip.

Boxers used thongs too, with a piece of sheepskin underneath. This protected their fists and saved them from bruising their knuckles. Didn't do much to protect the man they hit!

There were two kinds of **wrestling**. One was very like modern wrestling; to win, you had to throw the other man three times. The other kind of wrestling, called pankration, was more like all-in wrestling, and although there were rules, such as "No eye-gouging or biting", it was very violent and a lot of competitors got hurt.

The **long jump** was different from the modern event; the athletes had a weight in each hand, which they swung forward as they leapt.

In the **Pentathlon** the athletes had to be real all-rounders. They had to take part in discus-throwing, javelin-throwing, running, jumping and wrestling - all on the same afternoon.

There were **races** in a special area called the hippodrome. There wasn't a hippopotamus in sight, however - hippo is Greek for horse. The riders had no saddles, and stirrups were not invented until over 1000 years later. Chariot racing was popular too. Some chariots were drawn by horses, others by mules.

The prize for all this? Honour, glory and a laurel wreath. But when the winners got home they were excused from paying taxes and were often awarded special seats for life at their local theatres and stadiums. In Pylos, a pretty town in Greece, you can still see the fine house of one successful athlete. It's the very best house in the town, so you know it certainly paid to win the Olympics!

PAIN OR POISON, SIR?

Did you know, the earliest anaesthetic *(that's a pain killer)* was described by Homer in his story Odyssey, back in 830 BC. Mandrake, hemlock and Indian hemp were drugs used - but if they got the amounts wrong, these could be killers, too!

USELESS INFORMATION:
HAPPY HIPPO

Hippopotamus is Greek for River Horse! Another famous Greek hippo, the ancient doctor Hippocrates has nothing to do with horses, but is often called the Father of Medicine. His name gives us the Hippocratic Oath. All doctors today must take this oath, to promise to do their very best to keep their patients alive.

WAR!

Each city-state had its own army. There was always a war going on somewhere in Greece. Every spring, each citizen would go and look to see if his name was on the public notice board for military service that year. If it was, he had to be ready to go to war at a day's notice.

When one city-state wanted to fight another, the priests sacrificed an animal to the gods, then examined its insides to see whether the local army was going to win the battle. If the answer was 'yes' *(and don't ask me how they knew; to most people one set of entrails looks more or less like another)*, they sent heralds to declare war.

It looks a bit iffy to me!

All Greek men learned to fight as part of their education. They mostly fought on foot. Thessaly and Boeotia were two city-states which had cavalry, but this was not usual, although horsemen might act as messengers and scouts. Each army would also have a small group of archers, and another of javelin throwers.

Cavalry became more important in the Hellenistic Period. Philip of Macedon and his son Alexander the Great were the first commanders to use foot soldiers - infantry - and cavalry together.

Page 2

Page 2

Page 2

Page 3

Page 7

Page 6

Page 6

Page 3

Page 11

Page 26

Page 22

Page 14

Page 26

Page 32

Page 34

Page 40

Page 40

Page 29

Page 31

Page 29

Page 16

Page 15

Page 29

Page 19

Page 38

Page 38

Page 31

Page 18

Page 19

Page 18

Page 38

THE LAST BEARER OF BAD NEWS

Page 36

Page 36

Page 37

Page 30

Page 19

Page 39

Page 33

Page 33

Page 33

Page 43

Page 42

Page 43

Page 33

Page 33

Page 26

Page 26

Page 35

Page 34

Page 5

Page 35

Page 5

Page 43

There was no "army issue" uniform or armour. Each soldier had to provide his own gear. Those who were too poor to do so joined the Navy instead and rowed the warships.

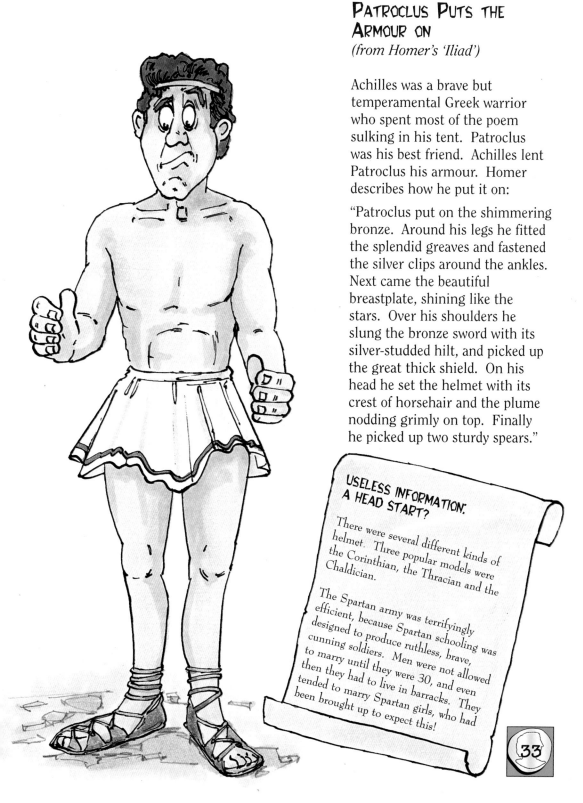

PATROCLUS PUTS THE ARMOUR ON
(from Homer's 'Iliad')

Achilles was a brave but temperamental Greek warrior who spent most of the poem sulking in his tent. Patroclus was his best friend. Achilles lent Patroclus his armour. Homer describes how he put it on:

"Patroclus put on the shimmering bronze. Around his legs he fitted the splendid greaves and fastened the silver clips around the ankles. Next came the beautiful breastplate, shining like the stars. Over his shoulders he slung the bronze sword with its silver-studded hilt, and picked up the great thick shield. On his head he set the helmet with its crest of horsehair and the plume nodding grimly on top. Finally he picked up two sturdy spears."

USELESS INFORMATION: A HEAD START?

There were several different kinds of helmet. Three popular models were the Corinthian, the Thracian and the Chaldician.

The Spartan army was terrifyingly efficient, because Spartan schooling was designed to produce ruthless, brave, cunning soldiers. Men were not allowed to marry until they were 30, and even then they had to live in barracks. They tended to marry Spartan girls, who had been brought up to expect this!

SHOULDER TO SHOULDER

Around 700 BC, Greek foot soldiers learned to fight shoulder to shoulder, in a tight formation called a phalanx. The man on your right protected you with his shield, and you did the same to the man on your left. It was hell being the man on the right hand end of the line!

Wait up a bit.
Just let me change
my weapon.

Soldiers like these were called hoplites. They had swords, but their main weapon was a spear for stabbing at some unprotected spot on his enemy's body. A good place was the neck, between breastplate and helmet.

As you can imagine, your shield was important, not only to you but to your mate on your left, because you protected him as well. A hoplite who ran away from the battle, and left his heavy shield behind so he could run faster, was bad news. So was one who came home without any blood on his spear. So a coward would dip his spear in a dead man's blood, and grab his shield, before coming home.

Two Last Stands

One of the most famous battles in ancient history was actually a defeat for the Greeks. But the losers were so brave that the Battle of Thermopylae (480 BC) has become more famous than some great victories.

The Persians invaded, and 300 Spartans blocked a narrow pass between the mountains and the sea. They could have held the pass for a long time against the whole Persian army, except that some of the Persians found a mountain track and sneaked up behind the Spartans while they were busy fighting off the main army. The Spartans were surrounded, but they fought grimly to the last man.

USELESS INFORMATION: NO COWARDS ALLOWED!

Greek women told their men, "Come back WITH your shield or ON it." This is because a warrior who threw away his shield and ran away was a coward. Dead heroes were carried home on their shields.

Now the Persians marched on Athens. Most people left the city and made for the ships *(a wise choice; they later hammered the Persians in a mighty naval battle, but that's another story)*. A few Athenians stayed on the hilltop of the Acropolis and rolled rocks down on the enemy. The Persian army climbed up the steep side of the hill and attacked. Some Athenians hurled themselves off the Acropolis to their deaths on the sharp rocks below. Others were slaughtered.

35

WAR AT SEA

If the Spartans had the best army, the Athenians had the best navy. In 483 BC they found a rich deposit of silver, which they used to pay for many things, including their fleet. They won many sea battles and kept enemies from invading their city. Their most famous sea battle against the Persians was at Salamis.

The crew of a ship were trained seamen, but the rowers were ordinary free men. Most were just too poor to buy armour and weapons to join the army. There were no galley slaves in the Athenian navy as far as we know.

The Athenian navy was partly paid for by rich citizens. 400 were chosen each year. Each had to keep one ship in good order. If he wanted to, he could go to sea in "his" ship and command it for that year!

The earliest warships were called penteconters and were rowed by 50 oarsmen. Later the bireme and the trireme were developed. Bi means two and tri means three; a bire me had two banks of oars on each side of the ship. A trireme, of course, had three.

The keel, below the ship, was made of seasoned oak for strength. The ship's timbers were from fir trees, for lightness. The sails were linen, controlled with ropes made of hemp or papyrus reeds. Two big oars were fastened at the back for steering. A thick rope ran under the keel. When it got wet, the rope became tighter. This helped to hold the ship's timbers together.

All warships had sharp bronze beaks in front, to ram other ships. They also had eyes painted in front to scare away evil spirits and to let the ship see where she was going!

The biggest warships were the triremes, with 170 rowers arranged in 3 banks, plus 10 officers, 14 foot soldiers and the captain. The bottom two rows of oars poked through portholes in the ship's sides. The top row rested on a wooden framework which stuck out from the ship's sides. All warships had an upper deck for soldiers to fight on. The tactics were to ram the other ship, or to scrape along the enemy ship's side with the sharp beak of your ship to try to break its oars, then try to board it and fight it out on deck.

Shipboard life was no holiday! Sleeping room was cramped. Cooking was dangerous because of all the wood around. However, warships did not usually have far to travel - it was the wider merchant ships which made all the long journeys, to trade with other lands.

SIEGE WARFARE

Sometimes an army would besiege a city. First they burned the crops in the fields to starve the people inside the city. Then they tried to surround the city so that new supplies of food or weapons could not come in.

Greek historians described some terrifying weapons. There were siege towers which could be rolled on tree trunks close to the city walls. Then men would fire arrows - sometimes aflame - into the city.

Catapults worked like giant bows, to fire javelins a long distance. There were simple battering rams made from great heavy logs, and some which ran on wheels and protected the men from anything the enemy slung at them.

Thucydides described a flame-thrower. It was like a wooden hut on wheels, which could be pushed close to the enemy's wall. Inside it were giant bellows which blasted air down a tube and into a big pot of burning tar. The flames from the burning tar were blown forward and would set fire to anything that would burn.

GODS AND GODDESSES

The Greeks had many gods. The Greek stories about them are like a mighty soap opera. As in a soap opera, the stories seem to go on for ever - the spotlight shifts from one character to another, and you have trouble keeping track of all the characters. Here's a brief cast list and the plot so far.

OLYMPUS - AN EVERYDAY STORY OF GODS AND GODDESSES

POSEIDON was the sea god. He and his brother Zeus fought for control of the sky. Poseidon lost, and in a sulk, he moved to an underwater palace. With one blow of his trident he could make earthquakes and storms, and sailors prayed to him for a safe voyage.

HADES, the god of the underworld, was another of Zeus's brothers. He usually stayed in his shadowy kingdom beyond the river Styx. His servants were Charon, the ferryman who rowed the spirits of the dead across the river, and the three-headed dog Cerberus, who guarded the gates of Hades's kingdom.

The rest of the gods lived in a beautiful palace above the cloud-covered top of Mount Olympus, eating ambrosia *(not rice-pudding)* and drinking nectar and having feuds with each other. Sometimes one of them would come down to earth and interfered in human affairs.

ZEUS was the ruler of the gods. He sent thunderbolts when he was displeased. He sometimes came to earth disguised as an animal or bird and made love to mortal women. For example, he wooed Leda disguised as a swan, and he showed himself to Europa in the form of a bull. These women then gave birth to great heroes - not surprisingly, as they were half human, half god. Zeus's queen was Hera, who was his third wife and also his sister *(and possibly mighty fed up with all of Zeus's mortal meddlings).*

PAN was the god of woods and pastures. He had goat's horns and ears, and hairy legs like a goat. He invented the pan-pipes, and protected shepherds and their sheep.

APHRODITE was the goddess of love and beauty, and Zeus's cousin. Her baby son Eros flew around shooting at people *(nice boy).* If an arrow pierced you, you would fall in love with the first person you met. He was said to be blind, which didn't help matters. Hera made Aphrodite marry Hephaestos and the pair were very unhappy.

DEMETER, Zeus's sister, was goddess of the earth and the harvest. Her daughter Persephone, the spring-goddess, was stolen by Hades and dragged down to the underworld to be his bride. After some hard bargaining, Persephone was allowed to return to Demeter, but only for half the year. That is why, according to the Greeks, nothing grows in winter - Demeter is sorrowing for her lost child.

ARES, the son of Zeus and Hera, was the god of war. He went to war with his two sons, Deimos and Phobos - Fear and Terror - and everyone hated and feared him.

ASCLEPIUS, Apollo's son, was the god of healing. He got into trouble with Hades for bringing the dead back to life.

HERMES, the messenger of the gods, was the son of Zeus and Maia, a giant's daughter. He carried a winged stick with two snakes twining up it *(as you do)*, and wore sandals with wings on.

DIONYSUS, the son of Zeus by Semele, a human princess, was the god of wine. He had an unfortunate start in life. When he was born, Zeus's wife Hera was so jealous that she ordered him to be torn to shreds and boiled in a pot. His grandmother rescued him and made him whole again.

HEPHAESTOS was Hera's son by Zeus, and he was so ugly that Hera was disgusted with him and threw him out of Heaven. Being a god, he could not be killed, but he was badly hurt and ever afterwards he was lame. Hephaestos was the craftsman of the gods, and he made many of the magic weapons in the Greek stories.

HESTIA, Zeus's elder sister, was a gentle goddess who protected the home and the family.

APOLLO was Zeus's son by a giant's daughter named Leto. He was the sun-god, and also the god of music, poetry, healing and sudden death. The moon was looked after by his twin sister Artemis, who also protected hunters and young girls.

ATHENE, the goddess of wisdom and also of Athens, was the daughter of Zeus by his first wife Metis. She protected all heroes and craftsmen.

41

SOME SCENES FROM THE ANCIENT GREEK SOAP OPERA

Here are the storylines for a few of the most famous Greek stories. Old Fishface, whose job was after all to teach us history, never had time to give us more than a few highlights. These highlights, however, were so exciting that there was a queue at the library to borrow the book.

THE FIRST SPIDER

Arachne boasted that she could spin and weave more skilfully than the goddess Athene. They had a competition, which Arachne won. Athene was furious. "You shall spin and weave all your life, wretched girl!" she cried. In a moment all Arachne's pretty hair fell out. Her face became tiny, with huge, glittering black eyes. Her body became small and black and her beautiful busy fingers changed into long, hairy legs...she was a spider. And, of course, the scientific name for spiders is Arachnidae!

THE GOLDEN TOUCH

King Midas wished that everything he touched would turn to gold. The god Dionysus granted his wish. "I warn you," the god said *(in an annoying-motherly way)*, "this will end in tears." But Midas was sure what he wanted. At first everything was wonderful -

within hours the king had a solid gold palace, a table laden with solid gold plates and cups and a garden full of solid gold plants. Then things went horribly wrong. Food and wine changed to gold as soon as they touched his lips. He hugged his little daughter, who became a lifeless golden statue. In despair, Midas begged Dionysus to undo the magic - and he did. "I hope you've learnt your lesson," he said. *(They had good script-writers in those days, too.)*

DONKEY'S EARS

Midas did not learn *his* lesson. He annoyed Apollo by saying the music of Pan's pipes was sweeter than Apollo's lyre. "There must be something wrong with your ears, Midas," said Apollo. He touched the king's head - and donkey's ears appeared.
Midas hid the ears with a scarf which he wound tightly around his head. He put the scarf on when he got up in the morning. He even slept in it, in case he needed to call a servant in the night. Headscarves became fashionable in the city. But Midas needed a haircut eventually, and his barber saw the ridiculous ears. He promised to keep the secret, but he kept thinking about the ears and laughing to himself. At last he was so desperate to tell someone that he whispered to the reeds on the river bank, "King Midas has donkey's ears!" And the reeds whispered the secret to everyone. The barber left the country in rather a hurry...

PERSEUS

As a baby, Perseus was cast adrift in a little reed boat; but he was rescued and grew up to be a great hero. Athene and Hermes helped him to cut off the head of the Gorgon Medusa. One glance from Medusa was enough to turn anyone to stone; but the gods gave Perseus a shield polished like a mirror. He used the shield like a driver's rear view mirror and so avoided looking at Medusa at all.. With their help he won magic sandals *(they didn't wear trainers in those days)* and a magic helmet and rescued the beautiful Andromeda from a terrible monster. He then had terrible trouble with his in-laws, but that's another story...

WORLD'S STRONGEST MAN

Heracles (or Hercules) was Zeus's son by a mortal woman and he was the strongest man in the world. He had many adventures, including holding up the earth to let Atlas, the giant who normally carried the world on his shoulders, take a rest. He is most famous for his twelve labours - twelve "impossible" tasks which he managed to complete, sometimes with the help of various gods, sometimes on his own. In the end his jealous wife tricked him into putting on a poisoned shirt. Heracles's flesh sizzled and burned and his blood boiled and hissed. Mad with pain, he built himself a funeral pyre and was burned alive.

43

FAIR PLAY

You've read about some rough behaviour in this book. Yet, in Athens, in the Classical Period, the rulers were very fair. Everyone had a say in how the city-state was ruled. *(That's the men, of course. Women didn't count here, either.)*
Our word Politics comes from the Greek word for city, polis.

Anyone could get up and have his say at the city Assembly. Poor citizens were paid a day's wages, so they too could take part in the government. In turn, rich citizens were expected to do something extra, such as paying for a play at a theatre. There was a lottery to choose 500 councillors who made decisions about the state.

USELESS INFORMATION.
COUNTDOWN!

Each speaker was allowed a fixed time, which was measured by a water clock. Water dripped from one pot into another. When the top pot was empty, the speaker had to stop. Some people think modern politicians should be made to keep to a time limit, too.

Fair trial?

If someone was accused of a crime, 200 jurymen would be chosen to listen to the trial. There were no lawyers. There were professional speech-writers to help the accused person to make his case. The jury listened, shouted, booed, hissed, asked questions. At the end they voted with little bronze discs.

Perhaps the biggest advantage of such a big jury was that it would be very difficult to bribe them!

USELESS INFORMATION – OSTRACISED!

An ostraca is a piece of broken pot. The Athenians wrote the names of officials they were not pleased with on an ostraca. If enough people did this, the unpopular official was ostracised and sent away for 10 years. You can probably think of several people who deserve the same fate...

45

MEANWHILE, IN SPARTA ...

Wouldn't you know it? In Sparta, they did everything differently. To start with, the Spartans got the local peasants to do all their farming for them. Then there were free men who did all the jobs in trade and industry. The cobblers and bricklayers, the blacksmiths and potters had no right to vote. The Spartans left all the everyday work to these guys. And off they went war-mongering.

The whole Spartan way of life was aimed at keeping the Spartans on top and the Helots and Periokoi down. They had a sort of secret police which hunted down troublemakers and killed them.

Hello. I'm a Helot and I give half my harvest to those lazy so-and-so's in Sparta.

I'm a Periokoi. Let 'em fight, I say. I'd sooner make pots.

At the age of 30, Spartan men were divided into "equals" and "inferiors". A vote was held to decide this, a bit like picking teams at school. Only equals could attend the assembly, where the people voted for and against proposals by shouting. Remember those game shows where the winner is chosen according to how loudly the people clap? Well, that's how the Spartans ran things.

From time to time, the Spartans banned all foreigners from their territory. This was probably because they were afraid of someone spying on them and telling enemies what they were doing. *(Of course, to the Spartans anyone who was not a Spartan was an enemy.)* A thoroughly rum lot, wouldn't you say?

47

A GREEK INVENTOR

Heard the one about Archimedes? He leapt out of his bath shouting "Eureka" *(which roughly translates as "Sorted!")*. He had discovered that if a plump Greek mathematician gets into a tub full of water, more water slops out than if a slender Greek maiden gets into the same tub *(though not at the same time)*. Even if his discovery never happened that way, the scientific principle worked - and still does.

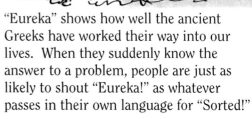

Other stories say Archimedes invented a crane which was based on land and swung out, grabbed enemy ships and capsized them. He also trained mirrors on enemy ships to set them on fire. Nobody knows how those inventions worked, or even whether they were ever used at all. They make good stories anyway. But one thing which Archimedes invented which is still used in many places today is Archimedes' Screw, which is a machine for lifting water from one level to another.

"Eureka" shows how well the ancient Greeks have worked their way into our lives. When they suddenly know the answer to a problem, people are just as likely to shout "Eureka!" as whatever passes in their own language for "Sorted!"

Words like politics, democracy, ostracism, phalanx, photograph *(literally, light-writing)*, alphabet, chorus, Olympics, Marathon, philosopher and stadium have all passed into English, together with the ancient Greek ideas they stand for. Ancient Greek stories are well known all over the world. Say "He has the Midas touch" or "It looks like a Trojan Horse to me" and people all over the world will know exactly what you mean.

Of course there is a great deal more to know about the ancient Greeks than one Sticky History can tell you. As Old Fishface would have said, you've seen the sweet shop window and tasted some of the goodies. Now go away and raid the shelves.